50 BRUTALLY HONEST TRUTHS OF LIFE

UNNATI SHAHI

Made with ♥ on the Notion Press Platform
www.notionpress.com

For the warriors battling life's storms, this book is yours. In its pages, find the raw truths we often dodge but desperately need. Here's to the fighters, the dreamers, and the survivors—may these truths be your armor and your light in the darkest of nights.

Contents

Contents

Contents

PREFACE

If you're tired of sugar-coated platitudes and ready for some real talk, then '50 Brutally Honest Truths of Life' can be your next read. This book doesn't mince words or sugarcoat reality. It's a straight-shooting guide to navigating the complexities of existence. From the blunt truth that happiness is a choice to the hard reality that success demands sacrifice, each page delivers unfiltered insights that will challenge and inspire you. If you're sugar-coating-proof and ready to face life head-on, grab a copy of this book and prepare for a no-nonsense exploration of what it truly means to live.

I

Happiness

*You are ultimately responsible for your own
happiness!*

II
Fairness

Life isn't fair, and it doesn't owe you anything.

III
Success

Success often requires hard work, sacrifice, and perseverance.

IV
Figuring Out

Nobody truly has it all figured out.

V
Failure

We all are gonna fail either sometimes or many times! Failure is an inevitable part of growth.

VI
Priority

You can't please everyone, so prioritize pleasing yourself.

VII

Time

Time doesn't care about your breakdown phases. It keeps passing on without waiting, so, better spend it wisely.

VIII
Past

Your past does not define your future.

IX
Change

Change is constant; adaptability is key to survival.

X
Excuses

Excuses won't get you anywhere. They are just escapes!

XI
Comfort Zone

Your comfort zone is a breeding ground for mediocrity.

XII
Trust

Trust is fragile; once broken, it's hard to rebuild!

XIII

It's Okay

Not everyone will like you, neither they will understand, and that's okay, stop hurting yourself to be a people-pleaser.

XIV

You

You are the only person you can control.

XV
Comparison

Beware, comparison can kill joy!

XVI

Money

Money can't buy happiness, but it can pay your medical bills, provide you food, let you study, or help you survive.

XVII
Explanation

No one owes you an explanation for their choices, but you owe it to yourself to understand your own motivations.

XVIII
Inner Dialogue

Your inner dialogue can either empower you or hold you back; choose your thoughts wisely.

XIX

Pain vs Suffering

Pain is an unavoidable part of life, but suffering is a choice we often make by clinging to our pain.

XX
Your Ego

Your ego can be your biggest obstacle, blinding you to your faults and preventing growth.

XXI

Vulnerability

Vulnerability is terrifying because it opens you up to rejection and hurt, but it's also the path to genuine connection and intimacy.

XXII

Best Things

The best things in life may be free, but they're also often the most overlooked and underappreciated.

XXIII
Messy Life

Life rarely goes according to plan;

It's messy, unpredictable, and chaotic.

XXIV
Material possessions

Material possessions and luxury provide temporary pleasure but often fail to fill the void within.

XXV

Toxic Comparison

Comparison is not only toxic but futile; there will always be someone richer, smarter, or more successful than you.

XXVI

Regrets

Regrets serve as painful reminders of the paths not taken and the opportunities missed; use them as fuel for growth.

XXVII

Fleeting Success

Success is subjective and fleeting, often leaving you feeling empty and unfulfilled once achieved.

XXVIII
Negativity

Negativity is contagious and addictive, poisoning your mind and soul if you allow it to fester.

XXIX

Perfection

*Perfection is an illusion that leads to
dissatisfaction and self-loathing!*

XXX

Fear

Fear is a primal instinct that often masquerades as rationality, holding you back from realizing your true potential.

XXXI
Your Mistakes

You are not defined by your mistakes, but by how you choose to learn and grow from them.

XXXII

Intuition

Your intuition is often forcibly drowned out by the noise of society and the demands of others; learn to listen to it.

XXXIII

The Greatest Risk

The greatest risk in life is not taking any risks at all, settling for a mediocre existence devoid of passion and purpose.

XXXIV

Reality

Your perception of reality is distorted by your biases, beliefs, and past experiences; strive for objectivity and clarity.

XXXV
Sweat & Bleed

You'll find that life doesn't hand out participation trophies for every little effort you make; sometimes, you'll sweat and bleed for a win, and that's the honest truth.

XXXVI

Self-image

Your self-image is a reflection of your inner world, a mirror that reflects back your deepest fears, insecurities, and doubts; love yourself, and watch as the world mirrors that love back to you.

XXXVII

Toxic People

Surrounding yourself with toxic people is a surefire way to poison your emotions and your own life.

XXXVIII

Fantasies

Dreams without action are just fantasies;

Roll up your sleeves and get to work.

XXXIX
Who's Responsible?

The only person responsible for your failures is staring back at you in the mirror.

XL
Leaking Roof

Ignoring your mental health is like ignoring a leaking roof; the damage only worsens over time.

XLI
Your Potential

Your potential is limitless, but so are your excuses.

XLII

Holding Grudges

Holding onto grudges is like drinking poison and expecting the other person to die.

XLIII

Your Plans

Life doesn't care about your plans; it laughs at your carefully constructed timelines and tosses them aside with a shrug. But, it cares about your actions!

XLIV
Loneliness

Loneliness can be felt even in a crowded room; it's a longing for connection that runs deeper than physical proximity.

XLV
Forgiveness

Forgiveness is not about excusing someone else's behavior; it's about freeing yourself from the shackles of resentment and bitterness.

XLVI

Obsession

Obsession can blind us to the beauty and richness of life, trapping us in a narrow tunnel vision of our desires.

XLVII
Decisions

Every decision we make carries consequences, some of which may not reveal themselves until long after the fact.

XLVIII

The Chains

Expectations are the chains that bind us, trapping us in a cycle of disappointment and disillusionment, until we learn to break free.

XLIX

Past Suffering

Your past suffering doesn't justify inflicting pain on others; break the cycle instead of perpetuating it.

L

Go For It!

Your story's an unfinished masterpiece; paint it boldly.

www.ingramcontent.com/pod-product-compliance
Lightning Source LLC
Chambersburg PA
CBHW031240130726

47988CB00008B/3169